Aa

actor

momathel ممثل

actress

momatheleh ممثلة

adult

kbeer كبير

aeroplane
US English **airplane**

tayara طيّارة

air conditioner

mukief مكيّف

air hostess
US English **flight attendant**

mudifeh مضيفة

airport

matar مطار

album

albom ألبوم

almond

luz لوز

alphabet

abjadeyah أبجدية

ambulance

سيارة إسعاف
sayarat iseaf

3

angel

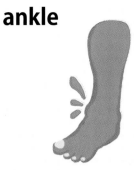

malak   ملاك

animal

haywan   حيوان

ankle

kahel   كاحل

ant

namleh   نملة

antelope

zabee   ظبي

antenna

aantain   آنتين

apartment

sha'a   شقة

ape

qurd   قرد

apple

toffaha   تفاحة

apricot

moshmosh   مشمش

apron

maryoul   مريول

aquarium

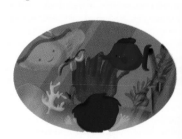

حوض سمك
hawed samak

English - Levantine Arabic

Designed and edited by : Maria Watson
Translated by : Ayman Khalaf

English - Levantine Arabic
My First Picture Dictionary

© Publishers

ISBN: 978 1 908357 98 4

Published by
Biblio Bee Publications
An imprint of **ibs BOOKS (UK)**
56, Langland Crescent, Stanmore HA7 1NG, U.K.
Tel: 020 8900 2640, Fax: 020 3621 6116,
email: sales@starbooksuk.com, www.starbooksuk.com

First Edition : 2018

Printed at : Star Print-O-Bind, New Delhi-110 020 (India)

This dictionary has been published in the following languages:
Arabic, Bengali, Bulgarian, Chinese, Croatian, Czech, Farsi, French, Gujarati, Hindi
Hungarian, Italian, Korean, Latvian, Levantine Arabic, Lithuanian, Pashto, Polish
Portuguese, Punjabi, Romanian, Russian, Slovak, Spanish, Tamil, Urdu and Vietnamese.

archery

rimayeh   رماية

architect

مهندس معماري
mohandes me'mary

arm

eid   ايد

armour
US English **armor**

dre'   درع

arrow

sahem   سهم

artist

fannan   فنان

asparagus

halyoun   هليون

astronaut

rajol fada'   رجل فضاء

astronomer

aalem falak   عالم فلك

athlete

ryadee   رياضي

atlas

كتاب خرايط
kitab kharayet

aunt

ammeh   عمّة

a b c d e f g h i j k l m n o p q r s t u v w x y z

author

mo'alef   مؤلف

automobile

sayyarah   سيّارة

autumn

kharef   خريف

avalanche

انهيار تلجي
enhyar thaljee

award

ja'ezeh   جائزة

axe

fa'es   فأس

Bb

baby

ولد صغير
walad sgher

back

daher   ضهر

bacon

لحم مقدد
lahem m'adad

badge

sharah   شارة

badminton

لعبة ريشة
le'bet reshah

bag

shentayeh   شنتاية

baker

khabbaz   خبّاز

balcony

balkoneh   بلكونة

bald

asla'   أصلع

ball

tabeh   طابة

ballerina

راقصة باليه
raqeseh baleh

balloon

baloon   بالون

bamboo

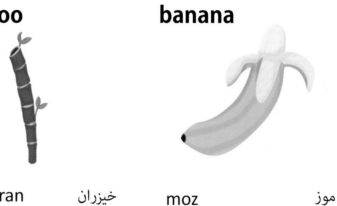

khayzaran   خيزران

banana

moz   موز

band

fr'a   فرقة

bandage

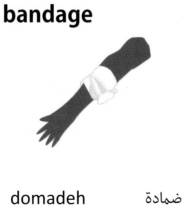

domadeh   ضمادة

barbeque

shway   شوي

a
b
c
d
e
f
g
h
i
J
k
l
m
n
o
p
q
r
s
t
u
v
w
x
y
z

barn

estabel   اسطبل

barrel

barmeel   برميل

baseball

لعبة البيسبول
lo'bet al-besboul

basket

salleh   سلّة

basketball

لعبة السلّة
lo'bet al-salleh

bat

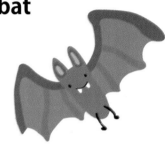

khaffash   خفّاش

bath

hammam   حمّام

battery

battareh   بطّارية

bay

khalej   خليج

beach

shate'   شاطئ

beak

min'ar   منقار

bean

fasoleyeh   فاصولية

bear

deb   دب

beard

da'en   دقن

bed

takhet   تخت

bee

nahleh   نحلة

beetle

khenefseh   خنفسة

beetroot

fejel   فجل

bell

jaeas   جرس

belt

hezam   حزام

berry

tot   توت

bicycle

بسكليته
besekleteh

billiards

belyardo   بيلياردو

bin

حاوية زبالة
hawet zbaleh

a b c d e f g h i j k l m n o p q r s t u v w x y z

bird

asfour   عصفور

biscuit

baskoteh   بسكوتة

black

aswad   أسود

blackboard

louh   لوح

blanket

ghata   غطا

blizzard

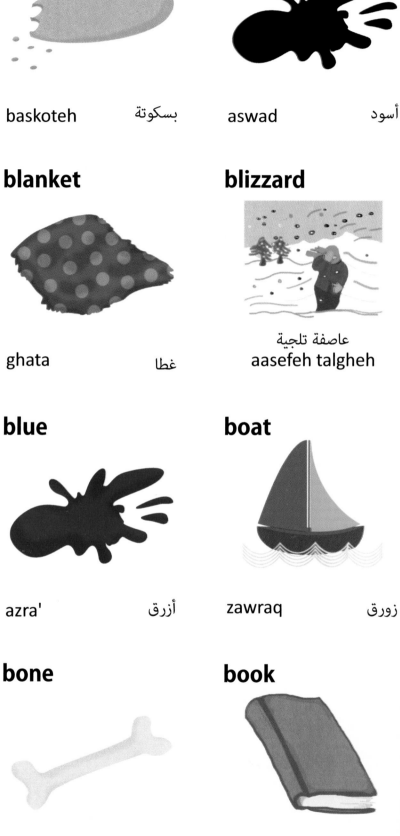

عاصفة تلجية
aasefeh talgheh

blood

dam   دم

blue

azra'   أزرق

boat

zawraq   زورق

body

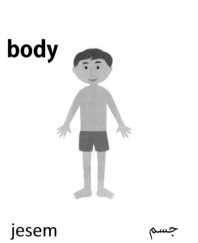

jesem   جسم

bone

admeh   عضمة

book

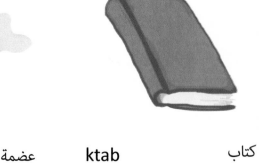

ktab   كتاب

boot

jazmeh جزمة

bottle

kaneneh قنينة

bow

o'deh عقدة

bowl

zebdeh زبدية

box

sandouk صندوق

boy

saby صبي

bracelet

iswara إسوارة

brain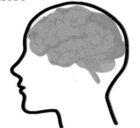

dmagh دماغ

branch

ghsen غصن

bread

khbz خبز

breakfast

ftor فطور

brick

blokeh بلوكة

bride

aroos   عروس

bridegroom

arees   عريس

bridge
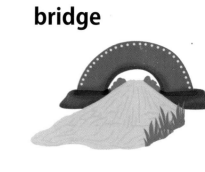
grser   جسر

broom

mkasheh   مقشة

brother

akh   أخ

brown

bonny   بني

brush

fershayeh   فرشاية

bubble

foka'a   فقاعة

bucket

satel   سطل

buffalo

gamous   جاموس

building

bnayeh   بناية

bulb

daw   ضو

bull

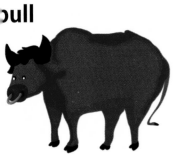

tor   تور

bun

ka'keh   كعكة

bunch

bakah   باقة

bundle

rezmeh   رزمة

bungalow

جناح صغير
jnah sagher

burger

humberger   همبرغر

bus

bas   باص

bush

شجرة صغيرة
shagara sghereh

butcher

lahham   لحّام

butter

zebdeh   زبدة

butterfly

farasheh   فراشة

button

rz   زر

a b c d e f g h i j k l m n o p q r s t u v w x y z

Cc

cabbage

malfof   ملفوف

cabinet

khzaneh   خزانة

cable

شريط كهربا
shreet kahraba

cable car

tal freak   تلفريك

cactus

sabbar   صبّار

cafe

cafeteria   كافيتريا

cage

kafas   قفص

cake

kato   كاتو

calculator

aleh hasbeh   آلة حاسبة

calendar

roznamah   روزنامة

calf

ejel   عجل

14

camel

gamal جمل

camera

camera كاميرا

camp

mokhayam مخيم

can

olbeh علبة

canal

kanah قناة

candle

sham'a شمعة

canoe

قارب صغير
kareb sagher

canteen

maksaf مقصف

cap

takeyeh طاقية

captain

kobtan قبطان

car

sayyarah سيارة

caravan

بيت متنقل
bayt motnakel

abcdefghijklmnopqrstuvwxyz

card

karet كرت

carnival

karnaval كرنفال

carpenter

najjar نجّار

carpet

sejjadeh سجادة

carrot

jazarah جزرة

cart

عرباية نقل
orbayeht nakel

cartoon

أفلام كرتون
aflam cartoon

cascade

shalal شلّال

castle

kal'a قلعة

cat

cata قطة

caterpillar

yarka يرقة

cauliflower

zahra زهرة

cave

kahef   كهف

ceiling

sakef   سقف

centipede

أم أربع وأربعين
om arba' w arba'een

centre
US English **center**

Al nos   النص

cereal

cornfleks   كورن فليكس

chain

selseleh   سلسلة

chair

kersee   كرسي

chalk

tabshora   طبشورة

cheek

khad   خد

cheese

jebneh   جبنة

chef

tabbakh   طبّاخ

cherry

karaz   كرز

a b **c** d e f g h i j k l m n o p q r s t u v w x y z

chess

shatrang   شطرنج

chest

sder   صدر

chick

soos   صوص

chilli
US English **chili**

فليفلة حدة
flefleh hadeh

chimney

mdkhaneh   مدخنة

chin

daken   دقن

chocolate

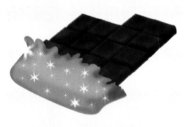

chokolah   شوكولا

christmas

عيد الميلاد
eid al-melaad

church

kneseh   كنيسة

cinema

cinema   سينما

circle

da'era   دائرة

circus

serk   سيرك

city

madeneh مدينة

classroom

saff صفّ

clinic

oyadeh عيادة

clock

sa'a ساعة

cloth

komasheh قماشة

cloud

ghemeh غيمة

clown

mohareg مهرج

coal

fahem فحم

coast

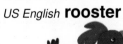

shate' شاطئ

coat

jacet جاكيت

cobra

cobra كوبرا

cockerel
US English **rooster**

deek ديك

cockroach

sarsour   صرصور

coconut

joz hend   جوز هند

coffee

kahweh   قهوة

coin

masaree   مصاري

colour
US English **color**

alwan   ألوان

comb

meshet   مشط

comet

mozannab   مذّنب

compass

bosleh   بوصلة

computer

computer   كومبيوتر

cone

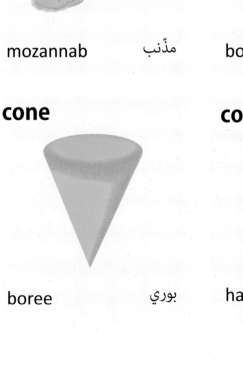

boree   بوري

container

hawyh   حاوية

cook

tabbakh   طبّاخ

cookie

betefour · بيتيفور

cord

habel · حبل

corn

arnous · عرنوس درة

cot

تخت ولد صغير
takhet walad sgher

cottage

kokh · كوخ

cotton

koton · قطن

country

balad · بلد

couple

zogen · زوجان

court

mahkameh · محكمة

cow

bakara · بقرة

crab

salta'on · سلطعون

crane

rafea'a · رافعة

a b **c** d e f g h i j k l m n o p q r s t u v w x y z

crayon

lon shame'   لون شمع

crocodile

temsah   تمساح

cross

saleeb   صليب

crow

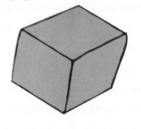

ghorab   غراب

crowd

zahmeh   زحمة

crown

taj   تاج

cube

moka'ab   مكعب

cucumber

khyar   خيار

cup

fenjan   فنجان

cupboard

khzaneh   خزانة

curtain

berdayeh   برداية

cushion

mkhadeh   مخدة

Dd

dam

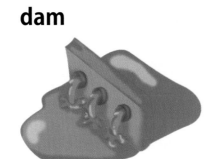

sadd   سدّ

dancer

raqes   راقص

dart

sahem   سهم

data

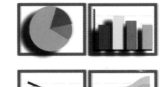

ma'lomat   معلومات

dates

tamer   تمر

daughter

ebneh   ابنة

day

yaoum   يوم

deck

ورق الشدّة
waraq al-shaddeh

deer

ghazal   غزال

den

areen   عرين

dentist

دكتور أسنان
doctor snan

23

a b c **d** e f g h i j k l m n o p q r s t u v w x y z

a b c **d** e f g h i j k l m n o p q r s t u v w x y z

desert

sahra   صحرا

design

tasmem   تصميم

desk

maktab   مكتب

dessert

tehlayeh   تحلاية

detective

mohakek   محقق

diamond

almas   ألماس

diary

yaomeyat   يوميّات

dice

zaher   زهر

dictionary
kamous   قاموس

dinosaur

denasour   ديناصور

disc

C.D   سي دي

dish

sahen   صحن

diver

ghatas   غطّاس

dock

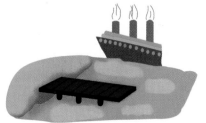

رصيف المينا
rasef al-mena

doctor

doctor   دكتور

dog

kaleb   كلب

doll

lo'eb   لعبة

dolphin

dolfen   دولفين

dome

kebbeh   قبّة

domino

domino   دومينو

donkey

hemar   حمار

donut

donat   دونت

door

bab   باب

dough

ajeneh   عجينة

dragon

tnen   تنين

drain

balo'a   بلوعة

drawer

daraj   درج

drawing

rasem   رسم

dream

mnam   منام

dress

festan   فستان

drink

aseer   عصير

driver

shofer   شوفير

drop

qatra   قطرة

drought

dawa   دوا

drum
drum
tabel   طبل

duck
batta   بطة

dustbin

US English **trash can**

حاوية زبالة
hawet zbaleh

duvet

mkhmal مخمل

dwarf

kazam قزم

Ee

eagle

saqer صقر

ear

eden ادن

earring

halak حلق

earth

الكرة الأرضية
al-kora al-ardeh

earthquake

zelzal زلزال

earthworm

دودة الأرض
dodet al-ard

eclipse

kosoof كسوف

edge

hafeh حافة

a b c d e f g h i j k l m n o p q r s t u v w x y z

eel

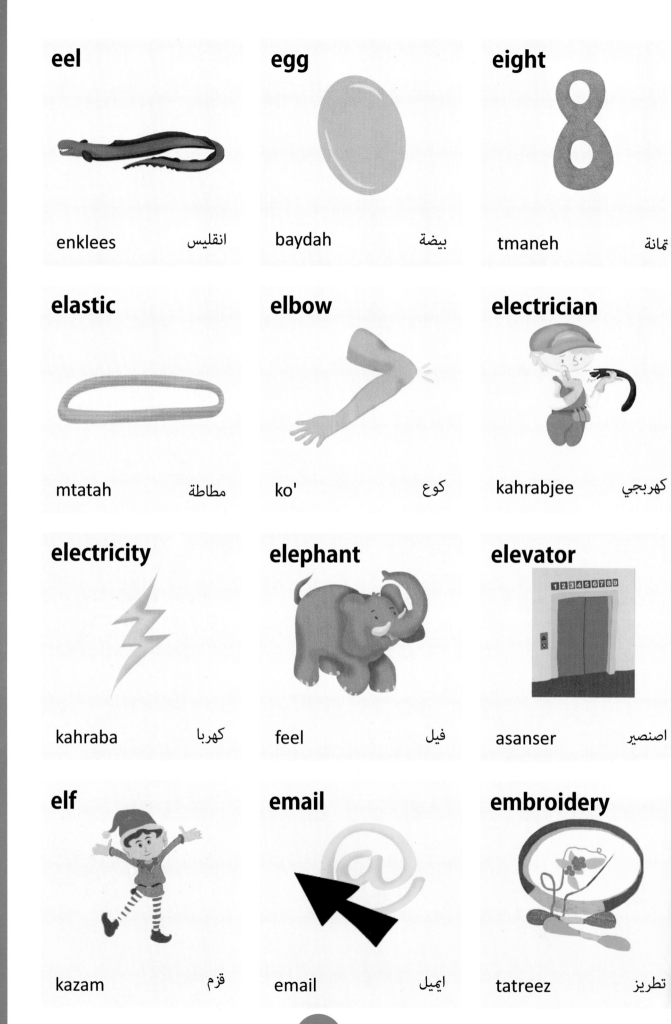

enklees   انقليس

egg

baydah   بيضة

eight

tmaneh   ﺛﻤﺎﻧﺔ

elastic

mtatah   مطاطة

elbow

ko'   كوع

electrician

kahrabjee   كهربجي

electricity

kahraba   كهربا

elephant

feel   فيل

elevator

asanser   اصنصير

elf

kazam   قزم

email

email   ايميل

embroidery

tatreez   تطريز

engine

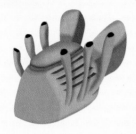

moharrek محرّك

entrance

madkhal مدخل

envelope

zaref ظرف

equator

خط الإستواء
khat al-estiwa'

equipment

adwat أدوات

eraser

mahhayeh محّاية

escalator

درج متحرك
daraj motharek

eskimo

askemo اسكيمو

evening

al-masa المسا

exhibition

ma'rad معرض

eye

ain عين

eyebrow

hajeb حاجب

Ff

fabric

naseej نسيج

face

wajeh وجه

factory

masna' مصنع

fairy

jneneh جنيّة

family

ayleh عيلة

fan

marwaha مروحة

farm

mazra'a مزرعة

farmer

fallah فلّاح

fat

smeen سمين

father

ab أب

feather

resheh ريشة

female

mara مرة

fence

syagh سياج

ferry

abbarah عبّارة

field

mal'ab ملعب

fig

teen تين

file

malaf ملف

film

film فيلم

finger

esba' اصبع

fire

nar نار

fire engine

سيارة إطفاء
sayaret etfa'

fire fighter

rajol etfa' رجل إطفاء

fireworks

al'ab ألعاب نارية

abcde**f**ghijklmnopqrstuvwxyz

fish

samakeh   سمكة

fist

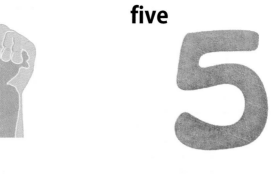

kabdah   قبضة

five

khamseh   خمسة

flag

alam   علم

flame

lahab   لهب

flamingo

flamingo   فلامنغو

flask

kaneneh   قنينة

flock

kate'   قطيع

flood

tofan   طوفان

floor

ared   أرض

florist

baya'   بياع ورد

flour

teheen   طحين

flower

wared   ورد

flute

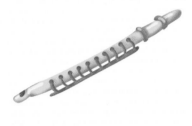

nay   ناي

fly

dbaneh   دبانة

foam

raghweh   رغوة

fog

dabab   ضباب

foil

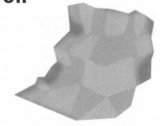

kasdeer   قصدير

food

Akel   أكل

foot

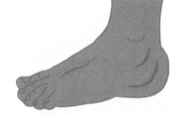

rejel   رجل

football

tabeh   طابة

forearm

sa'ed   ساعد

forehead

jbeen   جبين

forest

ghabeh   غابة

a b c d e f g h i j k l m n o p q r s t u v w x y z

abcdefghijklmnopqrstuvwxyz

fork
shokeh شوكة

fortress
kal'a قلعة

fountain
nafora نافورة

four
arba'a أربعة

fox
tha'lab ثعلب

frame
etar إطار

freezer
frezer فريزر

fridge
US English **refrigerator**
barad براد

friend
rfeek رفيق

frog
dofda' ضفدع

fruit
fawakeh فواكه

fumes
bokhar بخار

34

funnel

kame' قمع

furnace

fern فرن

furniture

faresh فَرش

Gg

gadget

aghezeh أجهزة

gallery

ma'rad معرض

game

lo'beh لعبة

gap

thaghra ثغرة

garage

karaj كراج

garbage

zbaleh زبالة

garden

jneneh جنينة

garland

tok wared طوق ورد

a b c d e f g h i j k l m n o p q r s t u v w x y z

garlic

tom   توم

gas

ghaz   غاز

gate

bawabeh   بوابة

gem

johara   جوهرة

generator

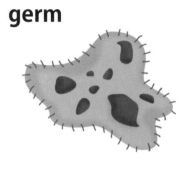

mwaldeh   مولدة

germ

garthomeh   جرثومة

geyser

hemmeh   حمّة

ghost

shabah   شبح

giant

omlak   عملاق

gift

hadeh   هدية

ginger

zanjabel   زنجبيل

giraffe

zarafeh   زرافة

girl

bnt بنت

glacier

galeed جليد

glass

ezaz إزاز

glider

طيارة شراعية
tayara shra'eh

globe

كرة أرضية
kora ardyeh

glove

kaff كفّ

glue

samagh صمغ

goal

goal غول

goat

anzeh عنزة

gold

dahab دهب

golf

golf غولف

goose

wazzeh وزّة

a b c d e f g h i j k l m n o p q r s t u v w x y z

gorilla
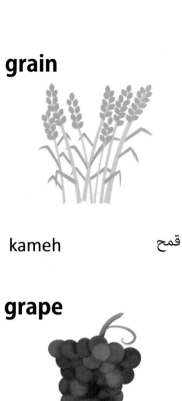
gorella   غوريلا

grain

kameh   قمح

grandfather

ged   جد

grandmother

tete   تيتة

grape

eneb   عنب

grapefruit

kreafoun   كريفون

grass

esheb   عشب

grasshopper

jondoub   جندب

gravel

bahes   بحص

green

akhdar   أخضر

grey

rmadee   رمادي

grill

mshwayeh   مشواية

38

grocery

خضرا وفواكي
khdra w fawakeh

ground

ared أرض

guard

hares حارس

guava

gawafeh جوافة

guide

daleel دليل

guitar

getar جيتار

gulf

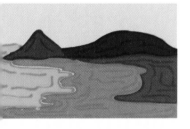

khaleej خليج

gun

sslah سلاح

gypsy

ghajareyeh غجرية

Hh

hair

sha'er شعر

hairbrush

فرشاية شعر
fershayet sha'er

a b c d e f **g** **h** i j k l m n o p q r s t u v w x y z

39

hairdresser

hallak حلّاق

half

nes نص

hall

ka'a قاعة

ham

لحم خنزير
lahem khanzeer

hammer

shakosheh شاكوشة

hammock

مرجوحة شبك
marjoha shabak

hand

eid إيد

handbag

shantet eid شنتة إيد

handicraft

صنعة يدوية
sen'a yadaweh

handkerchief

mahrameh محرمة

handle

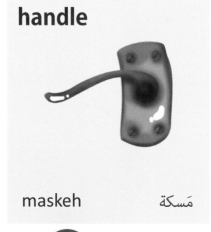

maskeh مَسكة

hanger

ieleka عليقة

40

harbour
US English **harbor**

mena   مينا

hare

arnab barry   أرنب برّي

harvest

mahsoul   محصول

hat

ta'eyeh   طاقية

hawk

saqer   صقر

hay

ash   قش

head

ras   راس

headphone

sama'at   سماعات

heap

komeh   كومة

heart

aleb   قلب

heater

sakhkhan   سخّان

hedge

syag shajar   سياج شجر

heel

ka'eb   كعب

helicopter

helcopter   هيليكوبتر

helmet

khozeh   خوذة

hen

jajeh   جاجة

herb

oshbeh   عشبة

herd

katee'   قطيع

hermit

nasek   ناسك

hill

hadabeh   هضبة

hippopotamus

فرس النهر
faras al-naher

hive

khaleyeh   خلية

hole

hofrah   حفرة

honey

assal   عسل

hood

ta'eyeh   طاقية

hook

sonnara   صنّارة

horn

karn   قرن

horse

hosan   حصان

hose

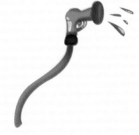

barbesh   بربيش

hospital

mstashfa   مستشفى

hotdog

nakank   نقانق

hotel

oteal   أوتيل

hour

sa'a   ساعة

house

bait   بيت

human

ensan   انسان

hunter

sayyad   صيّاد

a b c d e f g h i j k l m n o p q r s t u v w x y z

hurricane

e'sar اعصار

husband

zoj زوج

hut

kogh كوخ

Ii

ice

talj تلج

iceberg

jabal talji جبل تلجي

ice cream
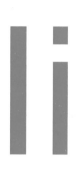
boza بوظة

idol
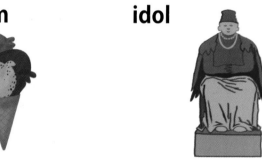
qudweh قدوة

igloo

كوخ الأسكيمو
kokh al-askemo

inch

inch انش

injection

ibreh ابرة

injury
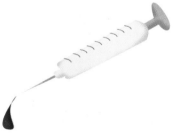
majroh مجروح

ink

heber حبر

inn

فندق صغير
fondo' sgher

insect

hashara حشرة

inspector

mofatesh مُفتّش

instrument

آلة موسيقا
aleh mosekeh

internet

internet انترنت

intestine

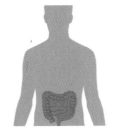

am'a' أمعاء

inventor

mokhtare' مخترع

invitation

da'weh دعوة

iron

yakwee يكوي

island

jazereh جزيرة

ivory

aaj عاج

Jj

jackal

wawi واوي

jacket

jaket جاكيت

jackfruit

kakaya كاكايا

jam

mraba مربى

jar

matraban مطربان

javelin

romeh رمح

jaw

fak فك

jeans

jenz جينز

jelly

jeleh جيليه

jetty

hajez mai حاجز بالمي

jewellery
US English **jewelry**

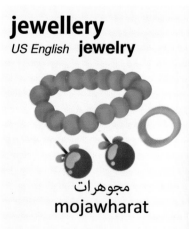

مجوهرات
mojawharat

jigsaw

pazel   بزل

jockey

fares   فارس

joker

moharrej   مهرج

journey

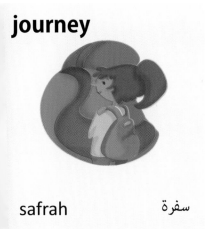

safrah   سفرة

jug

ebree'   إبريئ

juggler

mohtal   محتال

juice

asseer   عصير

jungle

ghabeh   غابة

jute

kheesh   خيش

Kk

kangaroo

kangher   كنغر

kennel

beit al-kalb   بيت الكلب

kerb
US English **curb**

حجر الرصيف
hajar al-rasef

kerosene

keroseen   كيروسين

ketchup

katchap   كاتشب

kettle

ghalayeh   غلاية

key

meftah   مفتاح

keyboard

kebord   كيبورد

key ring

حلقة مفاتيح
halaket mafateh

kidney

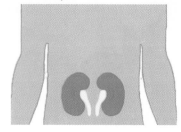

kleh   كلية

kilogram

kelo ghram   كيلوغرام

king

malek   ملك

kiosk

keshek   كشك

kiss

boseh   بوسة

kitchen

matbakh   مطبخ

kite

طيارة ورق
tayarah warak

kitten

kattah   قطه صغيرة

kiwi

kiwi   كيوي

knee

rekbeh   ركبة

knife

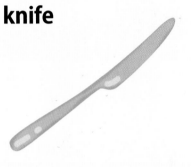

sekken   سكين

knight

fares   فارس

knitwear

treko   تريكو

knob

eid el-bab   ايد الباب

knock

tarek   طرق

knot

okdeh   عقدة

knuckle

مفصل الأصبع
mofsal al-esba'

a b c d e f g h i j **k** l m n o p q r s t u v w x y z

label

laska لصقة

laboratory

makhbar مخبر

lace

رباطات البوط
rabatat el-bot

ladder

sollom سلم

lady

marra مرة

ladybird

US English **ladybug**

zeez زيز

lagoon

bahra بحرة

lake

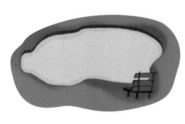

bahra بحرة

lamb

kharoof خاروف

lamp

labader لمبدير

lamp post

عامود ضو
amoud daw

land

ard أرض

lane

khat خط

lantern

fanous فانوس

laser

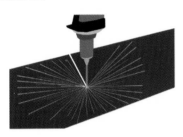

lazer ليزر

lasso

حبل صيد الحصان
haber sayed hosan

latch

kofel قفل

laundry

al-ghaseel الغسيل

lawn

osheb عشب

lawyer

mohamyeh محامية

layer

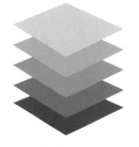

taba'a طبقة

leaf

ورقة شجر
wara'et shagar

leather

geled جلد

a b c d e f g h i j k **l** m n o p q r s t u v w x y z

leg

regel رجل

lemon

laymoun ليمون

lemonade

عصير ليمون
asseer laymoun

lens

adaseh عدسة

leopard

fahed فهد

letter

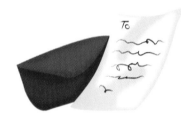

resaleh رسالة

letterbox

US English **mailbox**

صندوق الرسايل
sandouk rasayel

lettuce

khas خس

library

maktabeh مكتبة

licence

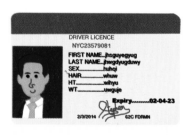

rokhsa رخصة

lid

gefn al-ain جفن العين

light

daw ضو

lighthouse

manara   منارة

limb
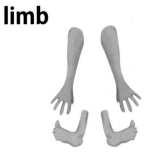
taraf   طرف

line

khat   خط

lion

asad   أسد

lip

sheffeh   شفة

lipstick

homrah   حمرة

liquid

sa'el   سائل

list

qa'emeh   قائمة

litre
US English **liter**

leter   لتر

living room

غرفة القعدة
gherfet al-ka'deh

lizard

sehleyeh   سحلية

load

hemel   حمل

a b c d e f g h i j J k **l** m n o p q r s t u v w x y z

loaf

rghef   رغيف

lobster

salta'on   سلطعون

lock

kofel   قفل

loft

s'efeh   سقيفة

log

قطعة خشب
kot'et khashab

loop

hala'a   حلقة

lorry

US English **truck**

shaheneh   شاحنة

lotus

louts   لوتس

louse

kamleh   قملة

luggage

ghrad   غراض

lunch

ghada   غدا

lung

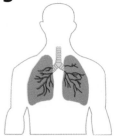

ri'a   رئة

Mm

machine
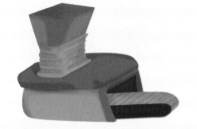
aleh   آلة

magazine

majaleh   مجلة

magician

saher   ساحر

magnet

mighnatis   مغناطيس

magpie

ghorab   غراب

mail

bareed   بريد

mammal

حيوان ثدي
haywan thadyy

man

rajoul   رجل

mandolin

mandoleen   مندولين

mango

manga   منغا

map

khareta   خريطة

a b c d e f g h i j k l m n o p q r s t u v w x y z

maple

al-kekeb القيقب

marble

rkham رخام

market

sou' سوق

mask

kena' قناع

mast

saryeh سارية

mat

hasereh حصيرة

matchbox

علبة كبريت
olbet kebriet

mattress

farsheh فرشة

meal

wajbeh وجبة

meat

lahmeh لحمة

mechanic

mikanik ميكانيكي

medicine

dawa دوا

melon

shamam   شمام

merchant

tajer   تاجر

mermaid

حورية البحر
horet al-baher

metal

ma'dan   معدن

metre
US English **meter**

meter   متر

microphone

mikrefon   ميكريفون

microwave

mekrefon   ميكروويف

mile

meel   ميل

milk

halleb   حليب

miner

عامل منجم
aamel manjam

mineral

ma'dani   معدني

mint

na'na'   نعنع

minute

دقيقة   da'e'a

mirror

مراية   mrayeh

mobile phone

موبايل   mobiel

model

عارضة   areda

mole

خلد   kheled

money

مصاري   masaree

monk

راهب   raheb

monkey

قرد   kored

monster

وحش   wahesh

month

شهر   shaher

monument

تمثال   temthal

moon

قمر   kamar

mop

mamsaha ممسحة

morning

sabah صباح

mosquito

namoseh ناموسة

moth

etteh عتة

mother

om أم

motorcycle

motor موتور

motorway

ostrad استراد

mountain

jabal جبل

mouse

fara فارة

mousetrap

mesyadeh مصيدة

moustache

shawareb شوارب

mouth

tem تم

a b c d e f g h i J k l **m** n o p q r s t u v w x y z

mud

teen   طين

muffin

kato   كاتو

mug

fenjan   فنجان

mule

baghel   بغل

muscle

adaleh   عضلة

museum

methaf   متحف

mushroom

feter   فطر

music

moseka   موسيقى

musician

moseke   موسيقي

Nn

nail

mesmar   مسمار

napkin

mahrameh   محرمة

happy
S English **diaper**

hafada   حفاضة

nature

tabe'a   طبيعة

neck

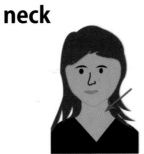

ra'beh   رقبة

necklace

too'   طوق

necktie

krafeh   كرافة

needle

ebreh   ابرة

neighbour
S English **neighbor**

jeran   جيران

nest

osh   عش

net

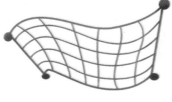

shabakeh   شبكة

newspaper

jaredeh   جريدة

night

lail   ليل

nine

tes'a   تسعة

a b c d e f g h i J K l m **n** o p q r s t u v w x y z

noodles

ma'karona   معكرونة

noon

وقت الضهر
wa'et el-doher

north
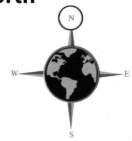

shamal   شمال

nose
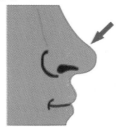

anef   أنف

note

molahazah   ملاحظة

notebook

دفتر ملاحظات
daftar molahazat

notice

balagh   بلاغ

number

rakam   رقم

nun

rahebeh   راهبة

nurse

momareda   ممرضة

nursery

hadaneh   حضانة

nut

mukasaraat   مكسرات

Oo

oar
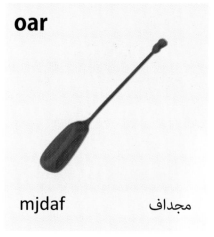
mjdaf   مجداف

observatory
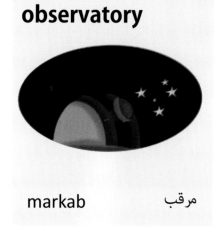
markab   مرقب

ocean
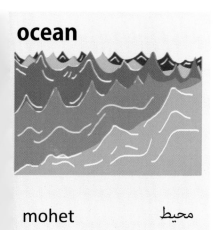
mohet   محيط

octopus

akhtabout   أخطبوط

office

maktab   مكتب

oil

nfet   نفط

olive

zaytoun   زيتون

omelette

بيض مقلي
bayed moklee

one

wahed   واحد

onion

basaleh   بصلة

orange

bort'aneh   برتقانة

a b c d e f g h i j k l m n **o** p q r s t u v w x y z

orbit

madar مدار

orchard

bostan بستان

orchestra

orkestra أوركسترا

ostrich
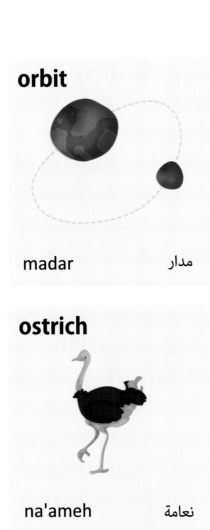
na'ameh نعامة

otter

kondous قندس

oval

baydawee بيضوي

oven

fren فرن

owl

bomeh بومة

ox

thor ثور

Pp

packet

rezmeh رزمة

page

safha صفحة

pain
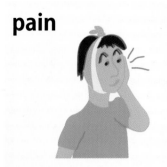
waja'   وجع

paint

dhan   دهان

painting

lawha   لوحة

pair

joz   جوز

palace

kaser   قصر

palm

kaf   كف

pan

moklayeh   مقلاية

pancake

ban kek   بان كيك

panda

banda   باندا

papaya

babaya   بابايا

paper

wara'a   ورقة

parachute

mzeleh   مظلة

parcel

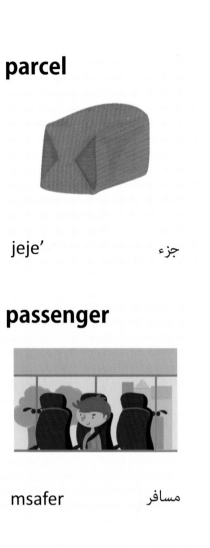

jeje'　　　جزء

park

hadeka　　　حديقة

parrot

babagha'　　　ببغاء

passenger

msafer　　　مسافر

pasta

ma'karona　　　معكرونة

pastry

mo'ajanat　　　معجنات

pavement

رصيف الشارع
rsef el-share'

paw

kaf　　　كف

pea

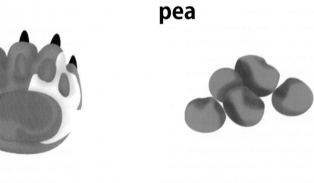

bazalyah　　　بزالية

peach

khokh　　　خوخ

peacock

tawoos　　　طاووس

peak

komeh　　　قمة

peanut

فستق سوداني
fosto' sodani

pear

enjas   انجاص

pearl

loleh   لولية

pedal

da'aseh   دعّاسة

pelican

baja'a   بجعة

pen

قلم ناشف
kalam nashef

pencil

kalam rsas   قلم رصاص

penguin

batreek   بطريق

pepper

folfol   فلفل

perfume

oter   عطر

pet

حيوان بيت
haywan bait

pharmacy

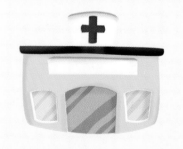

saydalieh   صيدلية

a b c d e f g h i j k l m n o **p** q r s t u v w x y z

photograph

sorah صورة

piano

byano بيانو

picture

sorah صورة

pie

ftereh فطيرة

pig

khanzer خنزير

pigeon

hamameh حمامة

pillar

da'ameh دعامة

pillow

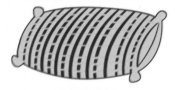

mkhadeh مخدة

pilot

tayyar طيار

pineapple

ananas أناناس

pink

zahre زهري

pipe

masorah ماسورة

pizza

betza   بيتزا

planet

kawkab   كوكب

plant

nabat   نبات

plate

sahen   صحن

platform

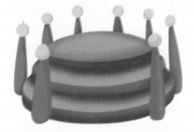

menbar   منبر

platypus

خلد المي
kheld al-may

player

la'eb   لاعب

plum

khokh   خوخ

plumber

معلم صحّية
m'alem soheyeh

plywood

رقايق خشب
raqayeq khashab

pocket

jebeh   جيبة

poet

sha'er   شاعر

a b c d e f g h i j k l m n o p q r s t u v w x y z

polar bear

db qutbee   دب قطبي

police

shorta   شرطة

pollution

talawoth   تلوث

pomegranate

romman   رمان

pond

brket may   بركة مي

porcupine

حيوان شوكي
haywan shawki

port

mena   مينا

porter

موظف مينا
mowazaf mena

postcard

مكتب بريد
maktab bareed

postman

بطاقة بريدية
beta'a baredeh

post office

ساعي البريد
sa'ey el-bareed

pot

tajoneh   طاجونة

potato

batata بطاطا

powder

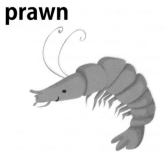

bodrah بودرة

prawn

jambari جمبري

priest

kahen كاهن

prince

amer أمير

prison

al-sejen السجن

pudding

boding بودنغ

pump

medakha مضخة

pumpkin

yakteen يقطين

puppet

lo'beh لعبة

puppy

jaroo جرو

purse

shentayeh شنتاية

a
b
c
d
e
f
g
h
i
j
k
l
m
n
o
p
q
r
s
t
u
v
w
x
y
z

quail

طير السمان
ter al-samman

quarry

makla' مقلع

queen

malikeh ملكة

queue

tabour طابور

quiver

shintayeh شنتاية اسهم

Rr

rabbit

arnab أرنب

rack

raf رف

racket

مضرب تنس
madrab tines

radio

radio راديو

radish

fejel فجل

raft

tof   طوف

rain

tomter   تمطر

rainbow

kos al-matar   قوس المطر

raisin

zbeb   زبيب

ramp
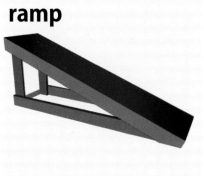
nazleh   نزلة

raspberry

tot   توت

rat

jardoun   جردون

razor

shafret   شفرة حلاقة

receipt

esal   إيصال

rectangle
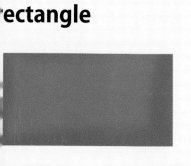
mostateel   مستطيل

red

ahmar   أحمر

restaurant

mat'am   مطعم

a b c d e f g h i J k l m n o p q **r** s t u v w x y z

a b c d e f g h i j k l m n o p q **r** s t u v w x y z

rhinoceros

وحيد القرن
wahed al-karen

rib

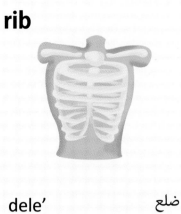

dele' ضلع

ribbon

sharet شريط

rice

rez رز

ring

halaka حلقة

river

naher نهر

road

tareq طريق

robber

harami حرامي

robe

roub روب

robot

robot روبوت

rock

sakhra صخرة

rocket

saroukh صاروخ

roller coaster

قطار الملاهي
ketar al-malahi

room

ghrfeh   غرفة

root

jazer   جذر

rope

habel   حبل

rose

wardeh   وردة

round

mdawar   مدور

rug

sejadeh   سجادة

rugby

كرة القدم الامريكية
koret al-kadam al-amrekeh

ruler

mastarah   مسطرة

Ss

sack

kes   كيس

sail

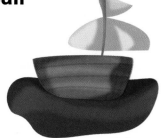

shera'   شراع

abcdefghijklmnopqr**s**tuvwxyz

sailor

bahar   بحار

salad

salata   سلطة

salt

melh   ملح

sand

ramel   رمل

sandwich

sanwish   صندويش

satellite

قمر صناعي
kamar senaie

saucer

صحن الفنجان
sahen al-fenjan

sausage

seje'   سجق

saw

menshar   منشار

scarf

lahsheh   لحشة

school

madraseh   مدرسة

scissors

mekas   مقص

76

scooter

skoter سكوتر

scorpion

akrab عقرب

screw

berghe برغي

sea

baher بحر

seal

fakmeh فقمة

seat

kersi كرسي

see-saw

قليبو جعيصو
kalebo ja'eso

seven

sab'a سبعة

shadow

zel ظل

shampoo

shambo شامبو

shark

koresh قرش

sheep

kharoof خاروف

shelf

raf   رف

shell

sodfeh   صدفة

shelter

maskan   مسكن

ship

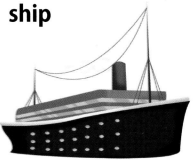

safeneh   سفينة

shirt

kames   قميص

shoe

bout   بوط

shorts

short   شورت

shoulder

ktef   كتف

shower

dosh   دوش

shutter

darfeh   درفة الشباك

shuttlecock

resheh   ريشة

signal

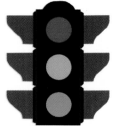

esharah   إشارة

silver

feddah   فضة

sink

magsaleh   مغسلة

sister

ekhet   أخت

six

seteh   ستة

skate

mezlaj   مزلاج

skeleton

هيكل عظمي
haykal azme

ski

tazalloj   تزلج

skin

bashara   بشرة

skirt

tannoura   تنورة

skull

jemejmeh   جمجمة

sky

sama   سما

skyscraper

ناطحة سحاب
natehet sahab

a b c d e f g h i j k l m n o p q r **s** t u v w x y z

slide

zehleta   زحليطة

slipper

shahata   شحاطة

smoke

dekhan   دخان

snail

halazoun   حلزون

snake

hayyeh   حيّة

snow

talej   تلج

soap

saboun   صابون

sock

jrabeh   جرابة

sofa

kanabayeh   كنباية

soil

trab   تراب

soldier

jendy   جندي

soup

shoraba   شوربة

space

fada'   فضاء

spaghetti

معكرونة
ma'karounah

sphere

جسم مدور
jesem mdawar

spider

ankabout   عنكبوت

spinach

sabanekh   سبانخ

sponge

esfanjeh   اسفنجة

spoon

ma'la'a   ملعقة

spray

bakhakh   بخاخ

spring

rabe'   ربيع

square

moraba'   مربع

squirrel

senjab   سنجاب

stadium

mal'ab   ملعب

stairs

daraj   درج

stamp

tabe'   طابع

star

najmeh   نجمة

station

mahatta   محطة

statue

temthal   تمثال

stethoscope

سماعة دكتور
sama'a daktor

stomach

me'deh   معدة

stone

hajar   حجر

storm

asefeh   عاصفة

straw

shalamoneh   شلمونة

strawberry

freazeh   فريزة

street

share'   شارع

student

telmez   تلميذ

submarine

ghawas   غواصة

subway

قطار كهربا
ketar kahraba

sugar

sekkar   سكر

sugarcane

قصب السكر
asab al-sukkar

summer

sayef   صيف

sun

shames   شمس

supermarket

سوبر ماركت
sober market

swan

baja'a   بجعة

sweet

helow   حلو

swimming pool

masbah   مسبح

swimsuit

mayo sbaha   مايو سباحة

a b c d e f g h i j k l m n o p q r **s** t u v w x y z

swing

marjoha مرجوحة

switch

كبسة الكهربا
kabset el-kahraba

syrup

شراب مركز
sharab mrakkaz

Tt

table

tawleh طاولة

tall

taweel طويل

tank

dababeh دبّابة

taxi

taksi تكسي

tea

shai شاي

teacher

estaz استاذ

teeth

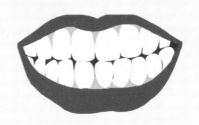

snan سنان

telephone

talefon تلفون

television

tefezyoun   تلفزيون

ten
ashara   عشرة

tennis
teniss   تنس

tent
khemeh   خيمة

thief
harami   حرامي

thread
khayet   خيط

three
tlateh   تلاتة

throat
hala'   حلق

thumb
ebham   ابهام

ticket
tazkara   تذكرة

tiger
nemer   نمر

toe
إصبعة الرجل
esba' el-rejel

abcdefghijklmnopqrst uvwxyz

tofu

al-toufo   التوفو

tomato

banadoura   بندورة

tongue

lsan   لسان

tool

adaah   أداة

toothbrush

فرشاية سنان
fershayet snan

toothpaste

معجون سنان
ma'joun snan

tortoise

sehefeh   سلحفة

towel

manshafeh   منشفة

tower

berej   برج

toy

lo'beh   لعبة

tractor

traktor   تراكتور

train

qetar   قطار

tree

shajara   شجرة

triangle

mothalath   مثلث

tub

hawed   حوض

tunnel

nafa'   نفق

turnip

lefet   لفت

tyre
US English **tire**

doulab   دولاب

Uu

umbrella

shamseh   شمسية

uncle

amm   عمّ

uniform

لباس موحّد
lebas mwahhad

university

jam'a   جامعة

utensil

أدوات مطبخ
adawat matbakh

a b c d e f g h i j k l m n o p q r s **t** **u** v w x y z

Vv

vacuum cleaner

مكنسة كهربا
maknaset kahraba

valley

wadi وادي

van

sayaret nakel سيارة نقل

vase

mazhareh مزهرية

vault

Khazneh خزنة

vegetable

khadra خضرا

veil

tarha طرحة

vet

دكتور بيطري
dactor baytary

village

karyeh قرية

violet

banafsajee بنفسجي

violin

kaman كمان

volcano

berkan   بركان

volleyball

الكرة الطائرة
al-kora al-ta'era

vulture

neser   نسر

Ww

waist

khaser   خصر

waitress

garsoneh   جرسونة

wall

heet   حيط

wallet

jezdan   جزدان

walnut

jouz   جوز

wand

عصاية الساحر
assayet el-saher

wardrobe

khzaneh   خزانة

warehouse

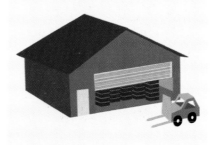

mostawda'   مستودع

a b c d e f g h i j k l m n o p q r s t u v w x y z

wasp

dabbour دبور

watch

sa'a ساعة

water

mai مي

watermelon

battekh بطيخ

web

shabakeh شبكة

whale

hoot حوت

wheat

kameh قمح

wheel

doulab دولاب

whistle

seffera صفيرة

white

abyad أبيض

wife

zawjeh زوجة

window

shebbak شبّاك

wing

janah   جناح

winter

shebbak   شتاء

wizard

saher   ساحر

wolf

ze'eb   ذئب

woman

mara   مرا

woodpecker

نقار الخشب
nakkar al-khashab

wool

souf   صوف

workshop

ورشة عمل
warshet amal

wrist

me'sam   معصم

x-ray

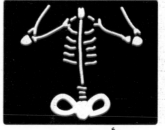

أشعة سينية
ashe'a seneyeh

xylophone

ekselefoun   إكسيليفون

a b c d e f g h i j k l m n o p q r s t u v w x y z

Yy

yacht

yakhet   يخت

yak

tor al-tbet   تور التبت

yard

jneneh   جنينة البيت

yellow

asfar   أصفر

yoghurt

laban   لبن

Zz

zebra

حمار وحشي
hemar wahshy

zero

sefer   صفر

zip

sahhab   سحّاب

zodiac

al-abraj   الأبراج

zoo

حديقة الحيوان
hadeket el-haywan